M000238273

Labrador Retriever

A Complete Pet Care Guide For Labs

Labrador Retriever breeding, diet, rescue, adoption, where to buy, cost, health, lifespan, types, care, and more included!

By: Lolly Brown

Copyrights and Trademarks

All rights reserved. No part of this book may be reproduced or transformed in any form or by any means, graphic, electronic, or mechanical, including photocopying, recording, taping, or by any information storage retrieval system, without the written permission of the author.

This publication is Copyright ©2016 NRB Publishing, an imprint. Nevada. All products, graphics, publications, software and services mentioned and recommended in this publication are protected by trademarks. In such instance, all trademarks & copyright belong to the respective owners. For information consult www.NRBpublishing.com

Disclaimer and Legal Notice

This product is not legal, medical, or accounting advice and should not be interpreted in that manner. You need to do your own due-diligence to determine if the content of this product is right for you. While every attempt has been made to verify the information shared in this publication, neither the author, neither publisher, nor the affiliates assume any responsibility for errors, omissions or contrary interpretation of the subject matter herein. Any perceived slights to any specific person(s) or organization(s) are purely unintentional.

We have no control over the nature, content and availability of the web sites listed in this book. The inclusion of any web site links does not necessarily imply a recommendation or endorse the views expressed within them. We take no responsibility for, and will not be liable for, the websites being temporarily unavailable or being removed from the internet.

The accuracy and completeness of information provided herein and opinions stated herein are not guaranteed or warranted to produce any particular results, and the advice and strategies, contained herein may not be suitable for every individual. Neither the author nor the publisher shall be liable for any loss incurred as a consequence of the use and application, directly or indirectly, of any information presented in this work. This publication is designed to provide information in regard to the subject matter covered.

Neither the author nor the publisher assume any responsibility for any errors or omissions, nor do they represent or warrant that the ideas, information, actions, plans, suggestions contained in this book is in all cases accurate. It is the reader's responsibility to find advice before putting anything written in this book into practice. The information in this book is not intended to serve as legal, medical, or accounting advice.

Foreword

The Labrador Retriever, or more popularly known as the Lab, has a long history of being man's best friend: a loyal companion to its owner, while also pulling its weight as a working dog. And no wonder, this large breed has a lot of energy to spare, and coupled with a high level of intelligence and a kind nature, this lovable dog has made its own place within people's homes and hearts.

If you have been thinking about keeping a Lab as a pet, or even if you are already the owner of a special Lab, it always pays to know as much as you can about them. From knowing more about the breed, its origins, tips for caring and training a Labrador Retriever, and their unique quirks and needs, this book can equip you to be the best owner of a Labrador Retriever that you can be!

Table of Contents

Introduction

Labrador Retrievers are arguably the most popular breed in the United States today. With their intelligent, endearing eyes and gentle, calm demeanor, they can be seen everywhere - rollicking around with the kids as a family pet, aiding persons with disability, helping law enforcement, or actively fetching game for their hunting owners.

While nobody can really say they "know" their pet, there have been time-tested and proven facts and quirks of the Labrador breed. And no wonder - they have been around humans since before they were officially recognized by the name "Labrador Retriever." Within these pages are some of those unique characteristics, qualities and peculiarities to Labradors and Labrador-ownership. Read on for tips or tricks in improving your relationship with your beloved Lab, or just to satisfy some curiosity you may have about the breed.

Glossary of Dog Terms

AKC – American Kennel Club, the largest purebred dog registry in the United States

Almond Eye – Referring to an elongated eye shape rather than a rounded shape

Apple Head – A round-shaped skull

Balance – A show term referring to all of the parts of the dog, both moving and standing, which produce a harmonious image

Beard – Long, thick hair on the dog's underjaw

Best in Show – An award given to the only undefeated dog left standing at the end of judging

Bitch – A female dog

Bite – The position of the upper and lower teeth when the dog's jaws are closed; positions include level, undershot, scissors, or overshot

Board – To house, feed, and care for a dog for a fee

Breed – A domestic race of dogs having a common gene pool and characterized appearance/function

Breed Standard – A published document describing the look, movement, and behavior of the perfect specimen of a particular breed

Buff – An off-white to gold coloring

Clip – A method of trimming the coat in some breeds

Coat – The hair covering of a dog; some breeds have two coats, and outer coat and undercoat; also known as a double coat. Examples of breeds with double coats include German Shepherd, Siberian Husky, Akita, etc.

Condition – The health of the dog as shown by its skin, coat, behavior, and general appearance

Crate – A container used to house and transport dogs; also called a cage or kennel

Crossbreed (Hybrid) – A dog having a sire and dam of two different breeds; cannot be registered with the AKC

Dam (bitch) – The female parent of a dog;

Dock – To shorten the tail of a dog by surgically removing the end part of the tail.

Double Coat – Having an outer weather-resistant coat and a soft, waterproof coat for warmth; see above.

Drop Ear – An ear in which the tip of the ear folds over and hangs down; not prick or erect

Entropion – A genetic disorder resulting in the upper or lower eyelid turning in

Fancier – A person who is especially interested in a particular breed or dog sport

Fawn – A red-yellow hue of brown

Feathering – A long fringe of hair on the ears, tail, legs, or body of a dog

Groom – To brush, trim, comb or otherwise make a dog's coat neat in appearance

Heel – To command a dog to stay close by its owner's side

Hip Dysplasia – A condition characterized by the abnormal formation of the hip joint

Inbreeding – The breeding of two closely related dogs of one breed

Kennel – A building or enclosure where dogs are kept

Litter – A group of puppies born at one time

Markings – A contrasting color or pattern on a dog's coat

Mask – Dark shading on the dog's foreface

Mate – To breed a dog and a bitch

Neuter – To castrate a male dog or spay a female dog

Pads – The tough, shock-absorbent skin on the bottom of a dog's foot

Parti-Color – A coloration of a dog's coat consisting of two or more definite, well-broken colors; one of the colors must be white

Pedigree – The written record of a dog's genealogy going back three generations or more

Pied – A coloration on a dog consisting of patches of white and another color

Prick Ear – Ear that is carried erect, usually pointed at the tip of the ear

Puppy – A dog under 12 months of age

Purebred – A dog whose sire and dam belong to the same breed and who are of unmixed descent

Shedding – The natural process whereby old hair falls off the dog's body as it is replaced by new hair growth.

Sire – The male parent of a dog

Smooth Coat – Short hair that is close-lying

Spay – The surgery to remove a female dog's ovaries, rendering her incapable of breeding

Trim – To groom a dog's coat by plucking or clipping

Undercoat – The soft, short coat typically concealed by a longer outer coat

Wean – The process through which puppies transition from subsisting on their mother's milk to eating solid food

Whelping – The act of birthing a litter of puppies

Chapter One: Understanding Labrador Retrievers

Labrador Retrievers are one of the most popular breeds today. Pictures of the lovable, cuddly puppies proliferate around the Internet, and the mature Labs are well-known for their calm and gentle temperaments, making them ideal pets for a family with children. Not only that, they are very visible everywhere as helping dogs - aiding persons with disabilities and helping law enforcement and emergency rescue teams. The Lab has had a long history of kinship, cooperation, friendship and family with humans. No wonder so many inevitably look to the Lab when they consider bringing home a pet.

But, as with any other pet, the perks and good times are balanced with the responsibilities of pet ownership. The Labrador, in particular, is a large dog and requires a lot of space. They will also need time and attention, as they are very social and require a lot of exercise. So before you make that decision of bringing a Labrador home, consider carefully whether or not you will be able to provide it with the right kind of home it needs.

Facts About Labrador Retrievers

Those cute and bouncy puppies can grow up to a sizeable adult. Labrador Retrievers are medium to large-sized dogs, characterized by a broad head with a pronounced stop, and slightly pronounced eyebrows. They have a broad and powerful chest and ribs, webbed feet and "otter"-like tails. These last two characteristics have been very useful to the Lab when he once worked as a fisherman's helper, fetching game for his owner - which oftentimes required swimming.

There are no recognized distinctions of types among the breed, but there are three coat colors that are officially accepted: black, chocolate, and yellow, and all three must be of a solid color, though there are, of course variations in the coloring, particularly of the yellow and chocolate variety. There is also a current debate regarding the controversial "silver" Labradors. Generally, the noses have the same color as the coat, and the eyes are usually brown or amber, with black lining around the eyes, and there is certainly no mistaking the intelligence behind those eyes.

Labradors have always been man's loyal helper, and their powerful build and physique help them in these tasks: they fetch game for hunters and for fishermen. Their powerful sense of smell allows them to detect dangerous or toxic substances, and their gentle nature and sheer loyalty has made them the beloved pets of many a person with disability who have found their pet's assistance to be priceless. All these responsibilities which many Labradors have taken on are a sign of their magnificent levels of energy and intelligence, which is why having a pet Labrador comes with the concomitant responsibility of providing them with proper training, exercise and care. If Labs are unable to work off their energy in some way, they will end up being destructive.

Labradors have been coexisting around humans for so long that they are very social and friendly, indeed. They have a kind and gentle nature, making them nonthreatening to kids and thus family-friendly. But because of this same social nature, they can be friendly even to strangers, which makes them unsuitable for guard dog duties. Also take note that their great need to socialize means that you cannot leave them alone for any long periods of time. Their natural bounciness and enthusiasm might get a bit awkward as they mature and grow in size and weight, but don't be too hard on them. That is just their natural joy at being around you.

The Labrador's average lifespan is 10-13 years. Proper care and nutrition can keep them healthy throughout their lives, and it is also important that they get a regular checkup with the veterinarian, and receive their annual shots. There are some genetic illnesses or diseases that can be passed down through the lines, which makes it important to be careful about breeding Labs. A perfectly healthy Labrador can be the delight of your family for his entire lifetime.

Like any large dog, however, Labs are prone to certain illnesses and conditions. These usually affect their joints, their bones and their eyes. Their energy levels might also be compromised with too much activity, thus causing muscular fatigue. If your Lab is prone to any of these conditions, bring them to a vet at the earliest opportunity to have them checked out. Even if it is a genetic condition, these can usually be managed by prescribed supplements and a change in their regular routines. The earlier these conditions are identified, treated and managed, the less likely it would grow to unmanageable proportions as your Lab grows older.

Summary of Labrador Retriever Facts

Basic Labrador Retriever Information

Pedigree: St. John's water dog, St. John's Dog, or Lesser Newfoundland

AKC Group: Sporting Group

Types: No distinction is made or considered standard among types

Breed Size: medium to large

Height: 21.3 to 22 inches (54-56 cm)

Weight: 55 to 80 lbs. (25 to 36 kg)

Coat Length: short and straight

Coat Texture: undercoat thick and soft, the overcoat a bit coarse

Color: black, chocolate and yellow (or other similar shades)

Eyes and Nose: brown and hazel eyes, nose will match the coat color

Ears: set slightly above the eyes and hanging close to the head

Tail: broad and strong

Temperament: friendly, kind, loyal, outgoing, gentle, friendly, may vary from calm and easy-going to enthusiastic and high energy, gets along well with children

Strangers: generally friendly, even to strangers, so do not make good watchdogs

Other Dogs: generally peaceful with other dogs

Other Pets: friendly and quite social

Training: intelligent and very trainable

Exercise Needs: very active; daily walk recommended; breed is likely to develop problem behaviors without adequate mental/physical stimulation

Health Conditions: obesity, progressive retinal atrophy, cataracts, hip and elbow dysplasia, anterior cruciate ligament tears, panosteitis, macular corneal dystrophy, myopathy

Lifespan: average 10 to 13 years

Labrador Retriever Breed History

Did you know that the Lab was once in very real danger of becoming extinct? The breed traces its origins to the St. John's water dog, which were active retrievers and hunter-dogs in Newfoundland. Their name "Labrador" actually began after they were brought to England around 1820, and were so named because they demonstrated their prowess as retrievers in the Labrador Sea. The name Labrador Retriever became known in 1870, where their popularity as retriever and hunting dogs became widespread in England.

Thankfully, they were so prized in England that the propagation of their breed was solidified in that country. When a sheep protection policy was promulgated in Newfoundland, coupled with a rabies quarantine in the United Kingdom, the St. John's water dog breed disappeared altogether in Canada. It can thus be said that all Labrador Retrievers in this day and age can trace their roots to their ancestors in the breeding kennels in England. Perhaps it is not really so difficult to understand the strong ties of loyalty and family that ties Labrador Retrievers and their human families.

The Labrador Colors

Kennel Clubs make no distinction among types in the Labrador breed, though they do recognize three official colors: black, chocolate, and yellow. It does seem that coat color is not a reliable distinction, because any and all three colors can manifest in a litter of Labrador puppies.

There are variations in these colors, of course. Yellow can range from a dark butterscotch color to lighter shades of yellow or cream. There have also been some manifestations of shades of gold and fox-red coat colors.

On the other hand, the chocolate-colored Labrador can come in varying shades of chocolate, while the black Labradors are of a uniformly solid color.

There has also been some controversy surrounding the silver or gray colored Labs, as many pet owners pushed for the acceptance of silver as a recognized and registered color. At this point, no official Kennel Club recognizes silver as a registered Labrador color, and there have been passionate arguments on both sides. Just as any litter can turn out puppies of all three colors, it seems that every so often, a gray or silver Lab also makes its appearance among the newly-borns. Enthusiasts are pushing for the recognition of silver as an official Lab color, but Kennel Clubs insist that there is no such thing, and thus must be the result of cross-breeding, negating the purebred status of silver Labs. The current controversy seems to point to the belief that silver Labs are actually the result of crossbreeding with Weimaraners. But as of this writing, the debate is still active and there has been no definite finding either way.

Chapter Two: Things to Know Before Getting a Labrador Retriever

After having learned some of the history and the unique nature and characteristics of the Labrador, there are a few other things you must ask yourself before making a final decision. Namely: what does it mean to keep a Labrador as a pet? Following are some practical facts and information around the pet ownership of a Labrador, including the cost of keeping one, licensing information, and the pros and cons of mixing a Labrador into your home and lifestyle.

Do You Need a License?

Expect licensing requirements to vary depending upon your location and the specific regulations or ordinances of the place where you live. The only real way to be sure is to do your research. Contact the local council of your area to inquire.

In general, however, most states in the United States do expect owners to register and license their dogs, and require proof of vaccination against rabies before granting you a license. Such licenses are renewed yearly, expiring at the same time as the vaccination. To renew the license, you also have to renew your Lab's vaccination.

The benefit of having a license is such that even if the state you reside in does not require licenses for dog owners, you might voluntarily wish to do so. Mainly, a license and registration properly identifies your dog so that if your Labrador ever gets lost, anybody can easily trace you as the owner, making it that much easier for your pet to find its way home.

How Many Labrador Retrievers Should You Keep?

While the answer to this would vary among prospective owners and their capacity for caring for Labrador pets, there are a few general standards you should keep in mine when thinking about keeping more than one Lab.

Labradors are large dogs, and so they require a lot of space. It has been said that the calm and gentle demeanor of Labradors make them suitable to keep in an apartment, but of course Labradors also have their energetic and restless days. Yes, Labradors are generally calm - provided they have been getting their regular exercise to burn off their seemingly inexhaustible amounts of energy. If you do not give them enough exercise, that energy can manifest in destructive behavior in your home, which would make you wonder why anybody ever thought of calling this breed calm and gentle to begin with.

If you decide to keep more than one, then having a reasonable-sized yard is necessary. Expect them to be playful and very social, so any rambunctiousness can play itself out in the yard instead of inside your home. Be wary also that the Lab's immediate environment is not littered with tiny objects within its easy reach. Lab's are insatiably curious, and they are eager eaters. That means that they will

put anything into their mouths, swallowing them even if
they are not edible. Make sure that their surroundings have
been "Lab-proofed," not only for cleanliness' sake, but also
for the safety and wellbeing of your pet.

More than one Labrador will easily translate into
double the cost of food and veterinary expenses, and
probably more than twice the amount of energy in grooming
and exercising them. Also be aware that mixing male and
female Labs might be a good idea for companionships' sake,
but unless you plan on breeding them, do the responsible
thing and have them neutered or spayed. Unless, of course,
you like the idea of being surprised by an entire litter of 7-15
little Labrador puppies just popping out one day.

Do Labrador Retrievers Get Along with Other Pets?

One of the reasons for the popularity of Labradors is
their kind and gentle natures. They will most likely get
along with other pets, and take the dignified higher ground
with other annoying housemates by being the tolerant giant.

How Much Does it Cost to Keep a Labrador Retriever?

Based on information gleaned from labs4rescue.com, the expected annual minimal cost for keeping one Labrador Retriever in the United States is set out in the second column of the table below. The third and fourth columns show a conversion of these base amounts into GBP and AUD, respectively. Please note that these basic conversions do not factor in the differing inflation rates per country.

Remember also that the following is just a minimal average estimate, and should therefore be reckoned with a wide allowance for other possible expenditures.

	In USD	based on conversion rate of 1GBP=1.438 USD	based on conversion rate of 1USD=1.303 AUD
License	$5-20	£3.47-13.91	AUD6.51-26.06
Collar, leash and tag	$20-50	£13.91-34.78	AUD26.06-65.15

Estimated annual food consumption	$325-750	£226.08-521.73	AUD423.47-977.25
Grooming supplies and services	$35-250	£24.34-173.91	AUD45.60-325.75
Pet Furniture	$50-200	£34.78-139.12	AUD65.15-260.59
Toys and other accessories	$100-300	£69.56-208.69	AUD130.30-390.90
Training in obedience schools	$75-300	£52.17-208.69	AUD97.72-390.90
Spaying or neutering	$50-225	£34.78-156.52	AUD65.15-293.175
Annual shots	$50-175	£34.78-121.73	AUD65.15-228.02
Medical care, treatment and supplements	$350-1,975	£243.47-1,373.89	AUD456.04-2573.42
Annual Total	$1,060-4,245	£737.38-2953.01	AUD1381.18-5531.23

So expect to have an average annual spending of $1,060 and upwards if you plan to keep one Labrador Retriever, not factoring in the initial cost of purchase if you decide to purchase one, or the cost of any destroyed furniture or items in the house.

What are the Pros and Cons of Keeping Labrador Retrievers?

Naturally, there are pros and cons to keeping Labrador Retrievers as pets. This is probably the best way of summing up all the above considerations to aid you in making your decision. At the end of the day, however, the question of whether a Labrador is a good pet to keep is something that each prospective owner has to answer on their own. Below is a list of possible factors you might think about as you consider both sides of the same dog.

Pros for the Labrador Retriever

- Endearing, sweet, playful and even-tempered dogs
- Intelligent and highly trainable, loves to please
- Friendly and easy-going

- Loyal, devoted, good with kids. A great family pet.
- Does not need excessive or complicated grooming and bathing, aside from regular brushing.
- A good pet for first-time dog owners since they are low maintenance, easygoing, and eager to please. Training should be easier compared to more independent breeds.
- Gentle and mild-mannered dogs, tolerant of the chaos of children in a busy household, so kid-friendly and make great family pets.

Cons for the Labrador Retriever

- A tendency to chew on and destroy furniture and other household items
- They shed. A lot.
- They are voracious eaters, which will lead to high costs of dog food if not unchecked, and also to an obese dog.
- Needs lots of exercise, which means that you will probably have to exercise a lot, too. Though this may be a pro for some very active owners.

If you're still coming down on the positive side, you might want to narrow it a little more by making a similar list as to whether you prefer a male or female Labrador. Though many times, this is a matter of personal choice and personal chemistry with your prospective pet.

Chapter Three: Purchasing Your Labrador Retriever

On Adopting Rescues

Before making a purchase, it is always a good idea to look into the possibility of adopting your pet from animal rescues or shelters. For one thing, it is less expensive, and you will also be doing the charitable thing by providing a home to a Labrador who needs it. And the choices may even be good ones: you might find a purebred Lab in need of rescue, perhaps even one that has already been trained and socialized. Or you may just find one that seems to speak directly to your heart.

Following are some informational resources providing listings or directories of Labrador rescues in the United States, the UK, and Australia

United States Rescues:

American Lab Rescue

A listing on Lab Adoption Resources from Golden Gate Retriever Rescue <http://www.labrescue.org/resources.html>

United States (US) Labrador Retriever Dog Rescues List <http://www.8pawsup.com/labrescues/>

New England Lab Rescue

Central California Labrador Rescue <www.cc-labrescue.org/available_list.php>

American Kennel Club Rescue Network <www.akc.org/dog-breeds/rescue-network/>

UK Rescues:

Labrador Retriever Rescue Southern England
<http://www.labrador-rescue.org.uk/>

Labrador Rescue (North West Area)
<http://www.homealabrador.net/>

Labrador Rescue (South East & Central)
<http://loveyourlabrador.co.uk/>

The Labrador Rescue Trust <http://www.labrador-rescue.com/>

The Labrador Lifeline Trust <http://labrador-lifeline.com/>

Labrador Rescue Kent & Borders
<http://www.labrescuekent.co.uk/>

A listing of Labrador Rescues from The Kennel Club
<http://www.thekennelclub.org.uk/services/public/findaresc
ue/Default.aspx?breed=2048>

Australia Rescues

Labrador Rescue
<https://www.petrescue.com.au/groups/10143?listings=reho
med&page=3>

Labrador Rescue <http://www.rescuealabrador.com/>

A listing of links to rescues on DogFoster
<http://www.dogfoster.org.au/vic.php>

These lists are just a starting point, of course. You should be able to expand your search from these lists, especially with online resources readily available.

How to Choose a Reputable Labrador Retriever Breeder

If you far prefer to purchase rather than to adopt, you should be willing to pay far more for a purebred Labrador puppy that has been medically certified. Online resources are rife with ready information to aid you in your search, and official Kennel Clubs usually carry a listing of reputable breeders.

Alternatively, you can also ask for leads from your local veterinarian, Kennel Clubs, or pet stores for their recommendations.

But finding them isn't the problem. The difficult part is making sure you are dealing with a trustworthy breeder who knows and uses the best practices in breeding Labs. You might start by asking them some general questions about the breed to see whether they are knowledgeable about the unique characteristics and needs of Labradors. Then you can ask for a tour of their facilities just to see that they are clean and healthy premises for the puppies. Don't limit yourself to one. Shop around, ask as many questions as you want, and satisfy yourself as much as possible on the qualifications and the condition of the newborn puppies. Feel free to ask about the puppies' mother and their sire, their health clearances, and how often and how many other litters they have produced. You want puppies with good genes, so an interest in the parents is only natural.

But don't take too long - being popular and high-in-demand pets, you can usually expect a long waiting list of willing prospective owners among reputable breeders. Ask about their payment schedules or preferences - place a deposit if necessary to make a reservation, and wait. Puppies are weaned fairly fast, so it shouldn't be a long wait.

Tips for Selecting a Healthy LabradorPuppy

You are lucky if you have the option of selecting your puppy from the litter, as puppies are usually reserved or booked way in advance. If you do have the good fortune of making your pick, here are a few pointers to aid you in selecting a happy, healthy and well-adjusted puppy:

- A glossy coat without any flaking of the skin.
- It should be alert, playful, attentive, reasonably active and well-fed.
- The eyes are clear and responsive, free of discharges

Ultimately, the choice of which puppy to pick is a personal one. After all, this little Lab will be your companion for the next 10-13 years, so some emotional factor in making your choice is okay, too. Labrador puppies have very endearing eyes, especially as puppies. You might find that the puppies ultimately end up choosing you.

Remember, however, that puppies must be fully weaned before you bring them home. This is usually not earlier than 8 weeks. They should be old enough by then to undergo complete separation from their mother.

Puppy-Proofing Your Home

When you bring a puppy home, it isn't just the puppy that would have to adjust to your lifestyle - you also have to make some accommodations and compromises to having a new living being in your home. And it isn't just the space they take up, or the time and attention that you will have to give to them. You also need to make sure that your home will be conducive to keeping a pet - for both their physical and mental wellbeing. Aside from having enough space for them to move and play around in, you should also make sure that your home is safe for your new friend.

Not unlike baby-proofing your home, puppy-proofing is similar in many respects. Perhaps there is a need for greater caution with Labs, whether adult or baby, because they will be moving around a lot faster than tiny toddlers. Their natural curiosity will lead them to explore and experiment, and the almost natural tendency of Labs to put many things into their mouths will mean that they are twice as more likely to get themselves into trouble.

Below are some things to be remember before you bring your Lab home:

- Keep all your medicines off the floor, safely stored in a well-sealed container or in the medicine cabinet.
- Don't leave small objects like kid's toys, tennis balls, or tiny candles within their reach. You may have been storing them somewhere in the bottom shelf of your cabinet where they wouldn't get in anybody's way. But now you have to keep them out of your pet's reach.
- Make absolutely certain that there is nothing poisonous or toxic within their reach. This would include plants, wallpaints, cleaning supplies, or even

any traps or poisons you may have laid out for any pests you've been trying to get rid of - whether in your house or in your yard. You certainly don't want to cause the poisoning of your Lab because of something that was intended to kill rats! And just because Labs are commonly used by law enforcement authorities to sniff out poisons doesn't mean you should assume that your Lab will know what's good for him or not. Those working dogs are trained, whereas your Lab is still waiting for you to train them.

- Make sure there aren't any live wires, dangling cords, open sockets or scattered wiring anywhere. The warning against poisons should apply also to the chances of electrocution. And even non-electric cords or strings or cables should be secured - you don't want your Lab getting tangled up and possibly even strangled because of sheer playfulness.

- Keep food items in proper containers and in storage. Remember that some human foods may not be good for your pet at all. And do remember to keep your garbage tightly secured.

- Secure your doors and windows - no matter how loyal they are, their natural curiosity will cause them to wander. If you have a yard, make sure it is surrounded by a fence that will be effective in keeping your pet from wandering out. Also secure fireplaces or any sources of open fire. And finally, secure any open containers of open water, such as swimming pools, drums or tanks.

- If you have puppies - close off stairwells to keep them from falling down the stairs, or from attempting to go up them.

This list is by no means exhaustive. Try to walk around your house and property once more, trying to see things the way a Lab would. You will probably find other possible sources of danger to them. Assume that, at some point or another, the Lab will have access to your entire house. In a way, it will be its house, now, too. Make it ready for your Lab, keeping their safety foremost in your mind.

Chapter Four: Caring for Your New Labrador Retriever

Take good care of them, and your Lab has the capacity to become your loyal and devoted companion for many years. So it is always a good idea to do your research - make yourself as much of an expert as you can about raising and caring for Labrador Retrievers. Read on for some basic tips about what makes a happy and healthy home life for your Lab, including their exercise needs.

Ideal Habitat for the Labrador Retriever

Labs are a gentle, kind, calm and even-tempered breed. With proper training, they can be adaptable to anywhere, even apartment living, though be aware that before they reach full maturity at around three years of age, they will still be a bit immature like puppies - with a lot of energy to spare! Be patient in training them, and once they've matured, you'll recognize the calm, gentle Lab everyone was talking about!

Ideally, however, Labs should have a yard to play in. Those bouncy puppies will grow to be bouncy adults, and unless you want them breaking delicate china or chewing furniture, better give them ample space to satisfy their curious nature.

The precautions in the previous chapter should be kept in mind. Fence in your yard - high enough to discourage them from jumping and escaping. Labs aren't usually diggers or jumpers, but they are extremely curious, and they can be very single-minded when the fancy takes them. This is another good reason why proper registration and licensing is important. While you may exert all effort to keep them safe and secure, sometimes they can just vanish! They should be traceable back to you if they do wander around, and being the registered owner will be a big help in many instances. Remember also that Labs are friendly animals - even to strangers. Be watchful with your Lab, just like you would be with any impressionable child, especially if you leave them in the yard for some time. An even better advice is to have a yard that is completely fenced-in, with a gate that you can lock.

Labs are very energetic and lively, but they also need their downtime. If you will offer them the run of your yard, give them a place where they can rest. A reasonably roomy dog house, equipped with a food bowl and water bowl that is constantly replenished - will give them shelter from the elements while giving them some space to take a quick nap.

If you let them sleep indoors, a dog bed will do. Train them not to sleep in your bed as early as possible, because this will be a difficult and discomfiting habit to outgrow once they begin maturing. On the other hand, offer them a reasonably comfortable dog mattress or pillow. Being large dogs, with a broad and full body and heavy bones, sleeping on a hard bed or on a cement or wooden floor can take its toll. As with many other large dogs, Labs are prone to conditions that affect their joints, bones and muscles. Prevent this from happening in the first place by giving them a warm and comfortable cushion with a firm support. It is the only right thing to do - particularly on cold and chilly nights.

One final thought is to allow him a sleeping area that is not constantly bombarded by lights or noise. Just like for any human, sleep is precious for dogs, too.

Exercise Requirements for Labrador Retrievers

Labradors need daily exercise. Forget weekend walks or walks to the park only when you have a day off from work or a free afternoon. If you don't have the time to provide them with daily exercise, then a Lab probably isn't for you.

This breed is a very active dog with lots of energy that needs to be released. Otherwise, they'll become restless and probably even destructive if kept indoors for long stretches of time. It is also important to provide them with sufficient mental and physical stimulation. Train them, or have them trained by a professional. In addition, they should be allowed to play - apart from their regular walks. Labradors Retrievers are - well, retrievers by nature, so a good fetching game should be very enjoyable to them.

They are also noted for being good swimmers - they are uniquely suited to swimming, with a waterproof coat, webbed feet, and an "otter" tail. The modern Labrador can actually trace their origins back to the St. John's water dog - a name which should speak for itself. These were fishermen's companions who used to haul nets and fetch game for their masters, diving right into the water to do so. With such a distinguished origin and background, why don't you let them test out their ancestry by letting them swim a few laps? And if you're worried about bringing home a wet dog - remember that their coats are water proof! All you probably need to do is give them a good rinse to wash off any accumulated chlorine, saltwater, or other substances that can severely dry their beautiful coats.

So invest in a good leash, and make sure their tags are properly attached to their collars. And when going out, especially during very active days in the summer, always remember to keep your dog (and yourself) properly hydrated.

Keeping Your Labrador Happy and Healthy

As the owner of a Labrador Retriever, it is your responsibility to keep your beloved pet happy and healthy. Feed them right, give them a good home, and give them enough mental and physical stimulation, and your pet should do fine. Be watchful for signs of illness, injury, or poor health, and always seek the help of a veterinarian in diagnosing those signs and symptoms. Being well-informed must always go hand in hand with the advice of a licensed professional.

Try to establish a set routine right from the beginning - from their meals to their regular exercise, right up to their weekly grooming needs. Not only does this teach them patience, it also regulates their body processes as to when meals are to be consumed and when energy is to be expended, with enough time for rest and play in between. Needless to say, such a routine is invaluable, especially when you are first housebreaking your Lab. Regularity is key.

Perhaps the most crucial advice for Labrador owners is to pay attention. Their needs can span anywhere from hunger to restlessness, or sometimes the simple need for affection and attention. Paying attention also helps you catch any illnesses or injuries as quickly as possible, and it allows you to become familiar with your Lab's unique individual traits and quirks.

Does he prefer retrieving and fetching more than swimming, for instance? Perhaps you can train him to fetch simple things about the house - Labs love to be useful, so being able to do something for you would make him happy, too. Does he tend to wander more than most Labradors? If so, you should probably keep a closer eye on him when he is in the yard for an afternoon - unless you're prepared to find the yard empty the next time you check on him! Is he a particularly beautiful specimen of his breed? Then maybe you can cultivate him to be a showdog to best show off his wonderful "colors," thus helping him to fulfill a role that he is uniquely suited for.

If he has a tendency to chew on things, no matter how hard you try to train him otherwise, perhaps you can simply acquire for him a sturdy chew toy. This can keep him happy while at the same time saving you from the discomfort of chewed-up furniture and the cost of having to buy new ones. If he is uniquely responsive to spoken commands, maybe you can try to see how many words he can recognize and obey? And if he seems to love your grooming sessions, you could probably invest in higher quality grooming tools.

Paying attention should also serve you in one more useful aspect: it reminds you that your Labrador is a unique and singular animal, and if you care for him, raise him and treat him properly, he can be a true best friend for many years to come.

Chapter Five: Meeting Your Labrador's Nutritional Needs

Labradors, more than most dogs, love to eat. This makes them especially prone to two conditions that Labs suffer from the most: obesity, and swallowing something inappropriate that needs professional medical services to treat.

Don't expect Labradors to be picky eaters, or even to know the notion of portion control. It is thus your responsibility as owner to make sure that he regularly eats right, eats well, and in proper proportions.

The Nutritional Needs of Dogs

Always make sure that your dog has sufficient drinking water readily available to himwhenever he needs to hydrate. Just like humans, a dog's body is mostly composed of water - which he can lose just as quickly through urination, sweating, and even drooling. They would need to replenish the water in their bodies, so find a good and heavy quality water bowl that will be less likely to overturn from your pet's playing around.

Following are some of the daily essential nutritional requirements that Labradors would need in their regular diet:

Proteins

Mainly obtained from meat and most meat-based products, protein is essential for growth and cell regeneration and repair, and for Labs especially, are necessary to help maintain their coat or fur. Be aware that experts do not recommend feeding your dog raw eggs, as this may have actually be harmful to their health.

Carbohydrates

This is usually derived from fiber-based products, and help in maintaining the intestinal health of your pet. Some carbohydrates can even be a good source of energy for your pet.

Fats

Fats provide your pet with a concentrated source of energy, and are also essential for some vitamins (A, E, D and K) to be absorbed. They help in protecting the internal organs and are vital in cellular production.

Vitamins and Minerals

Vitamins and minerals usually cannot be synthesized by a dog's body, so the primary source of these are the synthesized versions obtainable in commercially available quality dog foods. Vitamins and minerals help in the normal functioning of their bodies, and also helps maintain their bones and teeth.

How to Select a High-Quality Dog Food Brand

Start with reading the label: the first three ingredients listed will tell you whether it is a vegetable or meat-based dog food. Experts will tell you to choose the meat-based dog food over the vegetable-based one, even if it is more expensive. But don't make the mistake of thinking that you can substitute proper dog food with an all-meat diet. While being essentially omnivores, the important thing is to find balanced nutrition, which means essential vitamins and minerals, and not all of them are found in meat or meat products.

Opt for dry instead of canned dog food when you can, and limit feeding them table scraps. You don't want the possibility of having your Labrador suddenly come down sick with swallowing small bits of bone from the piece of meat, or fish bone from the fish you threw to him as a snack. And besides that, commercially available dog food have already been especially formulated for all of their daily recommended needs. Dry dog food should be fed regularly, to provide them with their daily proper nutrition. If you must feed them scraps, these should be as a treat, and not as a regular diet.

Understanding RER

RER, or Resting Energy Requirement, is the daily energy amount utilized by a dog while remaining at rest. If you have looked into this at all, you would know that there is usually a formula used to determine each dog's RER, and this is mostly based on their weight:

RER = 70 (weight in kg)$^{0.75}$

The idea is that, in the same way that we humans calculate our daily caloric intake based on our age, weight and activity levels, we can do the same for our dogs. For instance, if they become "active" (i.e., not resting), then their daily energy requirement also increases. These "activities" vary, and therefore so should the daily energy requirements. You would not feed the same amount to a neutered adult Labrador who is simply a house pet, for instance, compared to a pregnant Lab in her first few weeks of pregnancy. Below are some of the life changes that your Labrador might go through and a recommended adjustment in their daily RER:

Neutered Adult	RER x 1
Intact Adult	RER x 1.6
Moderate Work Adult	RER x 3
Pregnant dog in the last 21 days before birth	RER x 3
Weaning Puppy	RER x 3
Adolescent Puppy	RER x 2
Obese Puppy undergoing weight loss activities	RER x 1

While it may seem pretty straightforward, it actually isn't. Differences must also be accounted for breeds, the thickness of their coats, temperature, and other similar factors. You won't be feeding the same amounts to a Labrador Retriever, for instance, as you would to a pitbull. Among two Labradors with relatively similar weights, you won't feed them the same amounts if one is living in an apartment, as compared to one who has the free run of his family's backyard.

If you aren't sure, ask your veterinarian. Once you've established the best diet portion and schedule for your Labrador, the next best thing you can probably do is simply to pay attention. Does your Lab seem happy, healthy and with enough daily energy? Or is he hyperactive? Constantly tired and listless? Gaining weight or losing weight? Does he look like he's sick? Does it seem like he's losing his appetite? Adjust his diet accordingly, but only if it means slight increases or decreases in his usual daily meals. Don't make any drastic changes unless you have first consulted with a professional and referred your Labrador for a checkup.

Tips for Feeding Your Labrador Retriever

Diet needs will necessarily change over time, and you cannot expect to be feeding the same type or amount of foods that you give a puppy to a mature adult Lab. For that matter, you may also need to adjust their dietary requirements for their peculiar life changes, such as pregnancy, growing old, or being a "working dog." Even if your Lab is not a working dog, however, the level of activity he undertakes on a daily basis will determine, to a large extent, his daily dietary needs. Generally however, what determines how much a dog should eat is based on his weight and his daily activity level.

Consult with your veterinarian to determine the best daily food intake and feeding timetables for your pet, though you will also likely have to make adjustments for things such as weather, how strenuous their exercise regimen is, and possible periods of illness. Pay attention to the result: is your pet lethargic and lacking in energy? Perhaps you need to make adjustments, though always consult with a professional before making any drastic dietary changes.

Supplements are not to be given unless prescribed. If your Lab is in good health, it is better to err on the side of caution and avoid giving them additional vitamin or mineral supplements. If taken in too large doses, these may actually be harmful to your pet. Generally, these are prescribed only if your pet's weakened or ill condition requires it.

Over the past couple of years, there have been some attempts at formulating balanced and complete dog food that are homemade. Unless you are completely an expert on it - and unless you have the go-signal of your pet's veteriarian, it is advisable not to experiment. What may be perfectly fine to us is not always safe to eat for dogs. In fact, they could be downright toxic. Below is listed some "people food" that are not advisable to feed your Labrador:

Dangerous Foods to Avoid

According to the ASPCA, should your pet Lab ingest any of the following foods, you should probably bring them to a veterinarian immediately.

- Alcohol
- Apple seeds
- Avocado
- Cherry pits
- Chocolate
- Citrus
- Coconut
- Coffee
- Garlic
- Grapes/raisins
- Hops
- Macadamia nuts
- Milk and Dairy
- Mold
- Mushrooms
- Mustard seeds
- Onions/leeks
- Peach pits
- Potato leaves/stems
- Raw meat and eggs
- Rhubarb leaves
- Salty snacks

- Tea
- Tomato
  leaves/stems
- Walnuts
- Xylitol
- Yeast dough

.

Chapter Six: Training Your Labrador Retriever

One of the most rewarding, and yet often overlooked facet of pet ownership is their training. As an owner, you want your Labrador to be the best Labrador that they can be, to harness their intelligence and natural skills as much as possible. This is especially true for the Labrador, whose skills and intelligence have long been accepted as fact.

Labradors have a long history of "usefulness" to humans, being right there with their master to help with work. While the ancestors of the modern Labradors were retriever dogs - useful during hunting and fishing activities, nowadays they have branched out their skill set indeed. Labradors are one of the preferred breeds who serve as aids and companions to people with disability, and they have also been quite visible as sniffing dogs aiding law enforcement authorities.

Maybe you will never have to ask your Lab to help in bringing home the bacon, but surely you want them to maximize their potential as much as they can. In this chapter are some tips and guides on how to train your Labrador.

Socializing Your New Labrador Puppy

Socialization should begin as early as possible - with simple things such as spending time with him so that he can become accustomed to your presence and that of other humans. Experts caution that the window for effective socialization of puppies ends at 12-18 weeks. The Labrador puppy has a natural tendency to be cautious of anything new or strange, and unless addressed, it might become a permanent fixture of their character. After 18 weeks, it is almost impossible to belatedly introduce social skills. It is imperative, therefore, that you as the owner start giving them attention as soon as possible.

The main thing is that he becomes so familiar with you that he no longer views you - or anything new and strange - as a threat. This would also help shy puppies to develop more confidence. Playing with him, socializing in general, and creating a happy and positive environment in his association with you should go a long way in helping him develop those "people" skills. After all, the rest of their lives will be spent in the company of humans and in human environments, and a lack of the proper adjustment skills will create a shy or fearful Labrador constantly living under stress.

Begin introducing him to the world - take him out to the park or go for a walk, and just introduce him to new experiences. Again, it is important that it be a positive and pleasant experience for the puppy, until he learns that the wider world is not so threatening after all.

After you have made sure that your puppy has the basic social skills to grow into a well-adjusted Labrador, it is time to follow through with some obedience training. Start with some of the basics: housebreaking, not chewing on furniture, and obeying basic commands such as sit, come, and follow.

Below are some tips and tricks you can use as you start teaching your Lab these new skills:

Positive Reinforcement for Obedience Training

Labradors are uniquely lovable becaus they are so enthusiastic, intelligent, and eager to please. They will do the work expected of them - and eagerly, too - provided you teach them what to do in a patient and positive environment.

Positive reinforcement works in conjunction with punishment training, but don't think that any violence is involved. Because Labradors are so attuned to their owners' affection or lack of affection, positive reaction to positive behavior will reinforce that behavior, while negative reaction to undesirable behavior will teach them to avoid that behavior - they will not want to displease you. Negative reaction does not have to be anything violent - a simple refusal to show them affection for a time immediately after the undesired behavior will be enough. The immediacy of your positive reinforcement - or punishment after the targeted behavior will help them clearly identify which behavior is good and which is not good.

Remember that this is training - which means that it will necessarily have to be repeated again and again over a period of time. Much like a habit can only develop over time, the same can be true for pet training. Patience is always a virtue, and some firm and clearly recognizable discipline (such as by using simple and concise keywords) will, in the long run, teach your puppy better than mixed signals of lavish affection immediately after punishment.

Housebreaking Your Puppy

Many pet owners have their own unique ways of going about housebreaking their Labradors, and if it works for them and their pet, then it is effective. Perhaps you already have some idea of how to teach your Labrador not to go while inside thehouse. Sometimes something works, at other times they will not work. Keep in mind the principle of positive reinforcement above, and read on for some recommendations and suggestions on how to housebreak your puppy:

- You can try using a crate. At first create a sense of familiarity with the crate so that he is comfortable being inside it - whether to eat, nap or just play around. Gradually, you can confine him there for short periods of time, increasing the time he spends inside little by little. When the little Labrador can comfortably stay confined in the crate for about thirty minutes, leave him there at some point after meals until he does his business there. Praise him if he does. Reinforce the behavior.

- On the other hand, and this is useful if you do have the free run of your own backyard - regularly bring the puppy outside. Direct him towards the area of the yard where he can do his business, and keep him there until the deed is done. This should be done regularly, preferably at the same time and without fail until he willingly goes everytime you bring him to the same area at the same time each day.

- Confine your puppy to a select area of the house until he has become housebroken. It is important to create some familiar routines in the beginning - before you begin to allow him free access to the rest of your house. It is advisable to keep things simple in the beginning, and not to confuse them unnecessarily with new experiences and new surroundings, which can effectly dilute the training you are giving him.

The Working Labrador

While there aren't any recognized distinctions from within the breed, there are two recognized types of strains of Labradors.

The first are the Field Labs, or Working Labs, which thrive in America, and are generally more lithe, have longer legs, and are more agile. The other type is the Show Labs, or the English type, which are heavier in build and have thicker coats and tails. The latter have been bred mainly for beauty and for "show," and thus to adhere to conformation standards. The former are the true working dogs, which are often the ones more active in human activities. Though these physical characteristics are more the result of breeding and lifestyle, there are those who would advocate that depending upon which line your Lab comes from, your Lab has a greater propensity for either show or field work.

The lighter physique of the Field Labs obviously make them extremely suited to field work such as game retrieval and hunting activities, even swimming. But there is no such thing as exclusive work to the intelligent Labrador, and both types could be seen making their presence felt in both types of activities.

The range of work that Labradors can now take on have expanded considerably from their original hunter retriever duties. Because of their loyalty, patience and gentle natures, they are popular aid dogs, there to help people with various disabilities get around much easier in their daily activites. One recent development is the training of Labradors to become therapy dogs, which essentially capitalize on their cheerful, gentle and tolerant temperaments to lend some moral assistance people undergoing various kinds and stages of therapy.

Because of their strong sense of smell and determined focus when once they put their minds and resolve to accomplishing something, they have been put to good use by various law enforcement authorities for work such as sniffing out bombs or drugs or any other dangerous or illegal substances. They also assist in search and rescue operations by leading humans to those in need of emergency services and rescue. Needless to say, they have also been put to good use in searching for missing persons.

Also capitalizing on their strong sense of smell, Labradors have, more recently, been tapped as cancer-sniffing dogs.

But indeed the most common work for the Labrador is that which they were named for: retrieving. They help hunters by flushing out game from fields and brush, and when once the game has been shot and has fallen, they go after it to retrieve it and bring it back to its owner. The ability to hold the game in their soft mouths without damaging it is again a peculiar trait of the Labrador. But surely the ability to get the game and to bring it to its owner, without once being distracted or being tempted to play with or damage the little animal is a sure sign of its unique intelligence.

Provided proper training is given, of course. Past the stage when you are housebreaking your dog, and teaching him basic commands such as sit, stay, come, heel, and to play dead, there is the more intensive obedience training that comes with being a working dog. Much of it may stem from their desire to please their owners, but the range of what they can do indeed vary considerably.

Chapter Seven: Grooming Your Labrador Retriever

Labradors go through a process of molting, or shedding, which means that at regular intervals, you might find yourself dealing with a lot of dog hair in your house and on your furniture. Generally however, Labradors are considered low maintenance pets - from their origins as swimmers, they have dense, thick coats with its own natural oils that keep them considerably water proof. This coat is also effective in keeping them clean of dirt and mud and earth. But that does not mean that they do not need grooming. Labs also need regular brushing and grooming, and a regular examination of their entire body, including their eyes, ears, teeth, nails, to ensure that they are kept clean, healthy and disease-free.

Recommended Tools to Have on Hand

- narrow-toothed comb
- bristle brush
- dog nail trimmers
- a professionally-recommended ear cleaner
- toothbrush and toothpaste

Tips for Bathing and Grooming Labrador Retrievers

If you are keeping a Labrador as a pet, you already probably know that they shed or molt, thus their hair can get onto your clothes and furniture. This is perhaps the only real problem you can have with Labrador coats. With a history of being a great swimmer working alongside fishermen, the short and dense coat of Labradors are naturally water-resistant, and this generally keeps their coats free from accumulating dirt or debris.

Regular brushing is therefore advised, twice a week or so, mostly to help you deal with the shedding hair. This would also be an opportune time for you as owner and pet to get to know each other. Run your hands along their torso, legs, neck, ears and hindquarters, familiarizing yourself with the unique physique of your pet. Doing so regularly not only builds the bonds between the two of you and helps build on your pet's socialization skills, but you will also be able to catch any developing abnormalities such as injuries, wounds, bumps or any other oddities as quickly and as early as possible.

Labradors don't need constant bathing, either. Aside from the fact that their coat is naturally water-resistant, thus keeping them clear of the usual mud, dirt or filth that other dogs may pick up as a matter of course, but bathing too often will also strip their coat of the natural oils that serve to keep their coats shiny. Bathing twice a year is usually recommended, with water rinses every so often to keep his coat from drying, and just for the occasional general cleaning..

Use professionally prescribed dog nail clippers and ear cleaners. Because of the peculiar characteristic folds of the ears and muzzle of a Labrador, these places can accumulate quite a bit of bacteria. Unless cleaned regularly, it may become the starting point of viral illnesses or infections. Read on below for more information about these grooming tasks.

Other Grooming Tasks

Trimming Your Labrador's Nails

When your Labrador's nails begin clacking on the hardwood floor, it's probably time to give them a trim. This is necessary because dirt buildup under those nails may also cause infections. But more importantly, if they grow too long, they may catch on to things and be torn away, which would certainly be painful for your pet. That is why nail trimmimg is considered par for the course when it comes to grooming all dogs.

Use appropriate nail clippers - the ones suitable for dogs and the unique curvature of their nails. And be careful when you cut - the vessel that supplies blood to their nails is pretty close to the edge. If you cut their nails too short, you might cause bleeding and do the exact opposite of what you intended - to safeguard them from infection. If you arent' sure how to go about it, ask advice from your vet, perhaps even have them demonstrate it for you before you give it a try yourself. Done properly, trimming nails can keep your pet looking good and presentable and very clean indeed.

Cleaning Your Labrador Retriever's Ears

The best advice on this point is probably a negative: If you aren't sure how, don't. Let a professional do it. Dog's ears are sensitive, and they will most likely not appreciate you reaching in there to clean. If done improperly, you may actually do harm to your pet. Best to let professionals take over. Have them teach you how it's done while you're at it.

If you think this is something you'd like to do by yourself, however, read on for some general tips and advice on cleaning Labrador's ears:

- Use the appropriate tools. Do not use cotton swabs. It is safer for you to use plain cotton balls. Wash your hands prior to the cleaning. Or use gloves.
- Use the appropriate rinse. Do your research and find the right one for your pet. It shoud not contain any harmful chemicals, but it should also serve its purpose, which is to clean. Go online and research the products available. Better yet, ask your dog's veterinarian for his recommendation.

- Cleaning the dog's ears should be undertaken at least once a week. Clean the outer ears first, then work your way in. Don't force it, and be gentle. Use the cotton ball moistened by the rinse and just start cleaning.
- Above all, make this a positive experience for your pet. Once they realize that it isn't a painful or terrifying experience, they'll calm down once the weekly cleaning becomes routine.

Brushing Your Labrador's Teeth

Dogs aren't as fond of going to the dentist as most humans. So prevent them from getting tooth decay and gum disease in the first place. As always, prevention is better than any cure. And one of the ways to safeguard your Lab's dental health is by the regular brushing of their teeth.

Again, use the proper tools: dog toothbrush and toothpaste. It is best to start out when they are young to get them accustomed to the idea of their teeth being brushed. Proceed slowly. Like in any other training method, the secret is to be patient, and to gradually build the habit slowly over time.

At first you may want to start with the teeth that are within easy reach. Use gentle strokes so as not to injure their gums or cause them any discomfort. Over time, after a couple of weeks, you will probably be able to reach their full set of teeth. Once they see that there's nothing to fear, they'll tolerate, and probably even enjoy the process.

Aside from these regular weekly cleaning routines, keep them from having any undue tooth or dental problems in the first place: their food should give them adequate nutrition, and as much as possible, they should not be eating, chewing or digesting unhealthy or inappropriate things, such as painted wood blocks, or even sugary human foods like chocolate.

Chapter Eight: Breeding Your Labrador Retriever

The decision whether or not to breed your pet dog is a huge responsibility. And because Labradors generally have a huge litter, the responsibility is doubly more so. If you are thinking about breeding your Lab, the first thing you should probably do is ask yourself why you want to do so. Is it for commercial or monetary purposes, to somehow replicate your beloved pet, or because you feel it is only natural? Be warned that when you factor in the cost, breeding Labs for extra money is probably not worth it. You are also probably not going to create an exact replica of your beloved pet because each animal is unique. And while the breeding of any pet may be only natural, it is also incumbent upon owners to safeguard their pets against passing on or propagating hereditary or genetic diseases or disorders.

Learning Basic Dog Breeding Information

But if you are absolutely certain of your decision, then it pays to learn more about the process and what it would mean for you. How much will it cost? How much of your time and energy will it consume? Are you certain of the health of the dam and the stud? Are you willing to learn all you can about the process of dog breeding and reproduction, including possible complications, so that you are fully prepared for the occasion? If you are, remember that the process extends from the careful selection of breeders, the care for the pregnant Lab, the birthing process, and the weaning and care for the puppies, including securing a good home for all of them.

On the other hand, if you are certain that you do not wish to breed your Lab - which will likely be the case if they have been diagnosed with a genetic disorder, then it would be advisable to have them spayed or neutered. Having females spayed before their first heat may actually help to reduce their risk of cancer and other serious diseases.

Labrador Breeding Tips

Once the decision has been made to breed your Lab, the first thing you should do is have them checked out by a medical professional. Look around carefully for their prospective partner, and make sure that their medical condition is also optimal for breeding. Be selective and discriminating, and don't rush. Give yourself time to properly examine all the relevant papers and documents, including medical records. While you may not necessarily be looking for a "perfect" specimen, you must at least make sure that both are "clear" - that neither is a carrier for a degenerative condition or illness.

Once you find the right partner, the process itself should be pretty straightforward. Like most dogs, female Labs go through a period of heat,which also means that she is fertile or ovulating. This usually happens for the first time in a female Lab when she is about two years old, sometimes earlier. Many advise against breeding during the time of first heat, but to wait until the next or the following season to do so - then your pet is far more psychologically prepared for it.

Heat cycles can occur up to twice a year, every 6 or 7 months, and can last from around 14 to 21 days. The time of greatest fertility is around the 11th to the 15th day, which means that you will have to make preparations to keep both the male and female together during that time, or for about two weeks, ensuring proper socialization between them during that time. You will probably need to be watchful then, being ready to intervene if necessary, especially if it is the first mating process for either or both of them, and they might not know what to do or how to react.

The process itself starts with some socialization between the male and female, until the female shows that she is ready to accept the male. Once she accepts the male and the breeding process starts, it can last up to about forty-five minutes. It is advised for owners to be there to provide comfort and stability to the female Lab until the process is finished, especially if it is their first time, so that neither dogs suffer any injuries. Neither must the female be forced. A traumatic experience can severely impact their future breeding capacity. If successful, breeding can be repeated every other day to ensure a successful breeding, until the female no longer accepts the male.

Even if you are fairly sure that the breeding process is a success and that pregnancy has resulted, consult with a vet after 30 days to ensure that your pet is not simply manifesting symptoms of false pregnancy. Once you have gotten confirmation of pregnancy, you can begin to make preparations for the arrival of the puppies. In the meantime, take good care of your soon-to-be Labrador mother.

The gestation period can last to around 59-63 days. During that time, around the last five weeks, you should increase the portions of your dog's diet by about 20-50 percent to provide her with the proper nutrients as she nears the birthing date. By then, you should notice her demonstrating increased attachment to you as her owner, and a tendency to nest somewhere dark and quiet. By this time, you should have prepared a suitable sized bed or box for when she starts experiencing contractions and begins whelping.

There will be a drop in body temperature, usually down to 99 degrees from 101.5, some 24 hours before the birth is ready to begin. Try to take note of the time when the contractions start - these will manifest as "straining" which you can recognize if you place your hand near her abdomen. When you notice her begin to pant and breathe heavily, a puppy should not be far along. If she has started panting and there is no puppy within the next four hours, you might want to call a veterinarian. Typically, a puppy will be born around an hour and a half after the panting and straining has started. You will probably be asked at what time the contractions started, so it is useful to be attentive from the beginning.

Each puppy will come with its own after-birth, which is actually the placenta or the water sac. When being expelled from the uterus, this bag will burst, and the puppy will come out to take its first breath of air. The placenta should follow soon after. There are some mothers that will eat this after-birth, which can actually be a good source of protein and calories. Instinctively, the mother should also chew at the umbilical cord in order to free the puppy.

They will also lick clean their puppies, which should also stimulate the little ones to breathe and start crying. The entire birthing process could be as quick as two hours, or sometimes it can last for an entire day or more, with anywhere from ten minutes to an hour or more interval between puppies.

Throughout this entire process, you as the owner could provide your new mother with invaluable support. Particularly if it is a first-time mother, simply being there beside her, ready to offer her comfort and encouragement as she goes through the process could go a long way to calm her down. Mainly, though, you should allow her to undergo the process as naturally as possible, though you should be ready to intervene in certain instances. If the mother is taking too long to tear open the placenta, for instance, you could do this yourself. If there is any puppy not being licked clean and is not breathing, you can use a rough towel to clean the mouth and nose of the pup. Try, at least, to ensure that the puppy is not injured when the mother begins to chew and tear at the umbilical cord. And count the afterbirth. Each puppy should have one. If the number is off and one or two are missing, you should probably take your new mother to the vet. If there are any complications with the birth, call a vet. If it is a large litter and the birthing process is taking a long time, you can transfer some of the newborns to a different box lined with towels when the next contractions start. This will at least safeguard the little newborns from being stepped upon or caught up in the next contractions. You can place this box next to the mother, and in between contractions, they can begin nursing.

The newborn puppies should instinctively latch on to the mother's teats when they begin nursing. If they seem to be having trouble with this instinct, you can help them by placing their mouths next to the teat. It is imperative that they begin to nurse as soon as possible, so that they get the necessary nutrients and antibodies that will provide them with the mother's immunity for their first few weeks. This is the first milk from the mother, otherwise known as the colostrum. Also make sure that your mother is doing well, providing her with ready food and water to help replenish her energies.

Large breed dogs usually produce an average litter of 7 to 15 puppies, though of course this can be more or less. One interesting trivia about Labradors is that any color of the parents can result in a litter that consists of any or all the three recognized Lab colors of yellow, black or chocolate. Though it can take some time before pigmentation begins to manifest, particularly for the yellow Labs. Black Labradors are usually born with black skin

Raising Labrador Puppies

Puppies are blind and deaf at birth - they will have their eyes and ears closed. Always keep the litterbox clean - the lining should be changed regularly as urine and fecal matter can accumulate pretty quickly, especially after the third week. Make sure that your puppies are warm and clean, and keep them from being cold or chilled. If it is a large litter, you may have to supplement feeding them before it is even time to start weaning. You can use a bottle for this.

At around the 3rd or 4th week, the puppies will start being more active, which means you may have to secure a reasonably spacious area to keep them safely penned up. This is also the time when you begin to start weaning the puppies by providing them with solid food - preferably the brand of puppy food that you will be feeding them later on - moistened by water for their sensitive tongues and throats. Also provide them with water. Keep them away from unsafe or toxic objects - one of the recognized traits of Labradors is their propensity to swallow objects within their reach.

During the sixth week, they may be ready for solid food. By this time, you can bring them to the vet to get their first shots. Now that you are bringing them out into the greater world, the socialization process should also begin, though of course it has really started before that - within the litter itself. Encourage them and provide positive reinforcement for mingling and displaying amicable behavior to others.

They should be fully weaned at 5-6 weeks. This means that they can now survive apart from their mother, and it also means that the process of settling them into their new homes should already be underway. Unless you intend to raise and care for all of them - you will probably be looking for other prospective Lab owners. Ideally, this process should have already begun when your Lab became pregnant. If you had done everything right, you must now be able to proudly turn over a healthy puppy to its new owner.

Chapter Nine: Showing Your Labrador Retriever

While making great and loveable family pets, your Labrador Retriever can also show off its fine colors as a show dog. Keep them well-groomed and give them proper training to show off their intelligence. Then take a look at the requirements for the Breed Standard for Labrador Retrievers, which are the guidelines and criteria by which they are to be judged if entering a show, to determine whether your Lab has the makings of a great show dog. Then read on to discover more about what you will need to know to prepare your dog for show. Take note that the breed standard might vary slightly depending upon the country of origin of the hosting Kennel Club.

Labrador Retriever Breed Standard

General Appearance - A strong build, broad chest, ribs and skull

Temperament - Good-tempered, confident, kind, and shows a willingness to please, intelligent and biddable; shows of aggression or shyness result in a markdown

Head and Neck - A broad head with slightly pronounced eyebrows and a good strong neck, kind and expressive eyes of brown and hazel, with black lining around the eyes

Body and Tail - The body is powerful and muscular, with a distinctive "otter" tail.

Legs and Feet - Well-arched toes and well-developed pads, round and compact feet

Coat and Color - The registered colors are black, yellow and chocolate, and the coat is short and dense, and a slightly dry, oily coat, without wave or feathering

Size - Medium large; males from 22-24 inches tall at the withers, and females at 22-24 inches, each weighing from 65-80 lbs. and 55-70 lbs., respectively

Jaws and Teeth - Strong jaws and teeth with a regular and complete scissor bite

Gait - Free, covering adequate ground

Preparing Your Labrador Retriever for Show

If you think your Lab is a magnificent representation of the breed standard, then you can think about preparing them for the next dog show. Research the nearest Kennel Club in your area to determine their schedules and requirements, and then you can begin preparing in earnest.

Each pet owner may have their own unique ways and techniques of preparation, but here are a few general tips to keep in mind:

- Make sure you are fully aware of the requirements of the show; they can vary considerably from one area to another.
- Take your pet to the Vet and get a clean bill of health. Groom your pet, making sure they are on a proper diet and regular exercise to keep them at optimum

condition. Provide adequate physical and mental stimulation.

- Have you trained your Lab? You will probably need to give him some basic commands during the show, and of course being properly housetrained is important.

- Is he kind, affectionate and sociable? Displays of shyness, aggression, or even loud barking and whining may count against him. Test out his socialization skills, especially in a strange environment.

- Come to the show well-prepared, with all the various accessories, pet medication, toys, and grooming supplies that you will need. And make sure your Lab is well-rested, calm and relaxed for the big day.

Chapter Ten: Keeping Your Labrador Healthy

One of the reasons for the Lab's popularity among pet owners is because it is a low maintenance pet. Regular grooming, a proper diet, and regular exercise can be sufficient to keep your dog happy and healthy. And because the Lab is such a powerful and energetic dog, the need for regular exercise - on top of their daily walks - would help to prevent obesity - which the Labrador is particuarly prone to.

That said, there are a number of health conditions and problems which the Labrador Retriever can have, and the best thing that the pet owner can do is to stay informed about the causes and treatments. A regular visit to the Veterinarian can help you catch these conditions as early as possible before they worsen. But while it is always advisable to consult with a licensed professional to get a diagnosis, this chapter contains some general information about the common illnesses and conditions that can afflict Labrador Retrievers, so you will have some general idea of what to do when your Lab gets sick.

Common Conditions Affecting Labrador Retrievers:

There are two kinds of conditions that can affect your Lab. They can either be the result of genetic or environmental causes.

If it is genetic, you should consult with a licensed professional about any modern developments that address your pet's condition. If there are no cures, then you might at least learn of some ways of alleviating your pet's discomfort. But of course, this is after the fact. Many pet breeders caution pet owners against breeding dogs unless they have been given a clean bill of health, to ensure that no such similar genetic conditions are passed on to the puppies. Alternatively, aspiring Lab owners are advised to get puppies only from selected and reputable breeders, to ensure minimal risk of Labradors with negative traits.

The other type of conditions that can afflict your Lab are environmentally-related. These are caused by your pet's lifestyle: including their diet, the environment they move around in, and their daily routine. In most cases, catching these illnesses early on means that you can have them treated before they get worse.

Below are some of the types of illnesses that Labrador Retrievers can suffer from, including causes and possible treatment. Always remember, however, that a proper diagnosis can only be given by a licensed professional.

Common Health Problems Affecting Labrador Retrievers

Genetic Conditions

Hip Dysplasia

Hip Dysplasia can affect medium to large sized dog breeds. This is a condition which is caused by the malformation or improper development of the ball and socket portion of the hip, otherwise called subluxation. There is a loosening of the connecting tissue and ligaments in the hip, either on one side or both, that can gradually lead to loss of function and pain in the hip joints. The severity can vary among different dogs, and in some cases this can lead to osteoarthritis.

Not unlike with humans suffering from the same condition, the symptoms are pretty much the same: an ache or pain in the hip that can cause limping, inflammation, arthritis, all of which can result in decreased activity. Such symptoms can manifest itself in puppies of a few months old, though it can also show itself in older dogs, especially those suffering from osteoarthritis.

Most experts generally agree that genetics plays a big part in a Lab's predisposition to developing Hip Dysplasia. If either or both parents suffer from, or is a carrier of a line that suffered from, hip dysplasia, the puppy is at greater risk to developing the same condition. The same puppy also has a greater potential of passing on the same condition to its young ones later on.

There are surgeries that can be performed on Labrador Retrievers suffering from Hip Dysplasia, and have been carried out with good chances of success. However, the cost of such procedures can be prohibitive. Many pet owners can, however, help alleviate their pet's condition with various recommended treatments.

Hip Dysplasia can be severely worsened by obesity, which Labrador Retrievers are prone to being. Thus, proper diet is recommended, preferably one that has a good source of the recommended daily nutriets, calories and calcium. Thankfully, there are many available dog foods available that are specifically tailored to the Labrador's needs. Regular and daily exercise is also recommended, especially when your pet is growing up. Some of the recommended exercise includes swimming and running - particularlly because Labs are such great swimmers. Though moderation is advised: too little or too much exercise can actually worsen your pet's condition. For both diet and exercise, however, it is alway best to consult with a medical professional.

A medical professional can also provide your pet with any supplements, anti-inflammatories and pain relievers. You can also do your part by ensuring that their sleeping area and bed is warm and has the proper cushion and support, since a cold area or a chill is never good for arthritic states. Physical therapy threatments such as massages are also some of the possible recommended treatments.

Elbow Dysplasia

This condition is similar to Hip Dysplasia, except that it targets the elbow joints rather than the hips. The same treatments are also recommended.

Luxating Patella, or Patellar Luxation

Another genetic condition, though it may also be caused by trauma, this is a condition in which the kneecap becomes dislocated, or moves out of its normal position. Among larger dogs, Labrador Retrievers have a higher incidence of developing this condition.

Though it affects the knees instead of the hips, the symptoms, the diagnosis and possible treatment are also similar to those of Hip Dysplasia. The good news is that some Labs that suffer from a luxating patella do not feel pain. There is just a general stiffness that causes them to adopt a hopping or skipping gait, and a refusal to bend their leg until the surrounding muscles contract and the kneecap pops back into its usual position.

There are also surgical procedures that can address this condition, but you can manage it with proper diet and exercise, doctor-recommended dietary supplements and anti-inflammatories or pain relievers if needed.

Progressive Retinal Atrophy that may or may not lead to Cataracts

Yet another inherited disease, Progressive Retinal Atrophy or (PRA) is a slow and progressive condition that can happen over a number of years, leading to the eventual loss of sight. The early symptoms may be missed, though it generally consists of the loss of night vision or what is called night blindness. Since Labs have a strong sense of smell and hearing, they can use these other senses to navigate their way even when their eyesight is failing, thus making this a difficult disease to catch early on. You can also watch for dilated pupils and an increased shine in the eyes as a possible symptom. Refer to a Vet for proper examination, diagnosis, and the prescription of supplements.

There is no cure for this condition, and neither is there a widely successful treatment. Again, many specialists recommend a comprehensive ophthalmic examination prior to breeding your Labs, to ensure that no such condition is passed on to their puppies.

In the later stages of the illness, some pets may develop cataracts. While not all cataracts result from PRA, many Labs with PRA eventually develop cataracts. It is not recommended for a dog with a PRA-related cataract to get surgery, which is why it is so important to get a proper diagnosis. Some instances of cataract incidence in dogs can be treatable by surgery, but it is not advisable in all instances. In most cases, the only feasible treatment for a Lab with PRA is medically-prescribed supplements that can at least slow the progression of the retinal atrophy, and alleviate pain.

Retinal Dysplasia

This is another inherited condition that may result in poor vision, loss of vision, or blindness from birth. While there is no known cure, it is just possible that your pet may contract this illness due to prenatal infections such as herpesvirus and parvovirus, which is why it is so essential to give them all the necessary vaccinations.

Macular Corneal Dystrophy in Labrador Retriever

This is another condition that can affect the Lab's eyes, this time the corneas. It is usually not painful, though it impairs their eyesight. Carriers of this gene will not manifest the Dystrophy, but if both parents are carriers, chances are good that their pup will develop this condition.

Surgery is generally seen as the only possible treatment, though such procedures have not been very prevalent.

Hereditary Muscle Disease or Myopathy

This muscle disease is more commonly seen among yellow Labs, and is characterized by overall muscular weakness and a certain intolerance to exercise. Symptoms may include a predisposition to sitting or lying down or sudden collapse, all of which may be exacerbated by extreme temperature, or excessive exercise. This is obviously a difficult situation for a Labrador Retriever - a breed generally known for its great energy and strength, for whom a lot of exercise is generally recommended. If you suspect that your pet's energy levels is not normal, better have it checked by a professional - there are tests to verify whether or not your Lab has this condition. Otherwise, the daily routine and exercise you are giving your Lab is actually doing more harm than good.

Try to limit your pet's exercise and walk to moderate or light levels, and boost up their health with proper diet and nutrition.

Other Common Conditions

Obesity

This is perhaps one of the most common conditions affecting Labrador Retrievers, and the incidence of obesity among them can exacerbate other genetic predispositions, such as those affecting their bones, joints and muscle conditions (see above). And because Labs are also known for their great curiosity, which causes them to eat or swallow many of the things they come across, it isn't just obesity that results, but also emergency trips to the vet for having swallowed inappropriate objects. Obesity can also lead to heart conditions and diabetes.

Give your pet regular exercise, proper diet and nutrition, but most of all be watchful of their surroundings so that they don't keep eating objects or things that are not suitable for them. Labs like to eat, but it is also your responsibility to make sure they don't overdo it.

Panosteitis

Panosteitis is characterized by a sudden lameness among Labs from between the ages of 6 and 18 months, and may last from 2 to 3 weeks. This is also referred to as "growing pains," and is more common among large breed dogs.

Nobody knows what causes this condition, though thankfully it is not a permanent one. A visit to the vet might be appropriate, however, for the prescription of painkillers and to check that it isn't caused by infections or viruses.

Cruciate Ligament Rupture

This is an injury common among Labrador Retrievers, where the ligament in the knee tears, resulting in the lameness of the dog. Perhaps the reason why this is so prevalent among Labs is because of their great energy and their capacity for many heavy activities. Obesity may also contribute, if the knee ligament cannot support the dog's weight. In such a situation, it may not manifest as a sudden injury. Over time, the knee joint and ligaments may simply be stretched beyond its normal capacity until your pet suddenly begins limping.

If your pet suffers from such a condition, be sure to seek immediate treatment or surgery because otherwise it will lead to painful arthritis. And always remember that prevention is better than cure, so make sure to keep your pet on a regular, moderate exercise and a proper nutritious diet.

Preventing Illness with Vaccinations

Sometimes a Labrador Retriever's illness or disease can be prevented early on by proper vaccination. This gives them an immunity from contracting certain diseases, even when exposed to other dogs, such as parvovirus and distemper. There are shots that a puppy should be given before you even take him home, some recommended shots a few months later, and annual booster shots are recommended to help maintain his general immunity. Consult the table below for a general idea of what vaccinations should be given to your Lab, though take note that the schedule may often vary.

Vaccination Schedule for Dogs**			
Vaccine	Doses	Age	Booster
Rabies	1	12 weeks	annual
Distemper	3	6-16 weeks	3 years

Parvovirus	3	6-16 weeks	3 years
Adenovirus	3	6-16 weeks	3 years
Parainfluenza	3	6 weeks, 12-14 weeks	3 years
Bordetella	1	6 weeks	annual
Lyme Disease	2	9, 13-14 weeks	annual
Leptospirosis	2	12 and 16 weeks	annual
Canine Influenza	2	6-8, 8-12 weeks	annual

** Keep in mind that vaccine requirements may vary from one region to another. Only your vet will be able to tell you which vaccines are most important for the region where you live.

Labrador Retriever Care Sheet

Following is a quick Labrador Retriever care sheet that summarizes many of the information that has been provided in this book. The following pages will enable you to have quick grasp of all the information provided in this book, as well as a starting point for further research. At the very least, it covers some of the most salient points in owning Labrador Retrievers, which can enable you to quickly determine whether it is right for you to get a Labrador Retriever as a pet.

1.) Basic Labrador Retriever Information

Pedigree: St. John's water dog, St. John's Dog, or Lesser Newfoundland

AKC Group: Sporting Group

Types: No distinction is made or considered standard among types

Breed Size: medium to large

Height: 21.3 to 22 inches (54-56 cm)

Weight: 55 to 80 lbs. (25 to 36 kg)

Coat Length: short and straight

Coat Texture: undercoat thick and soft, the overcoat a bit coarse

Color: black, chocolate and yellow (or other similar shades)

Eyes and Nose: brown and hazel eyes, nose will match the coat color

Ears: set slightly above the eyes and hanging close to the head

Tail: broad and strong

Temperament: friendly, kind, loyal, outgoing, gentle, friendly, may vary from calm and easy-going to enthusiastic and high energy, gets along well with children

Strangers: generally friendly, even to strangers, so do not make good watchdogs

Other Dogs: generally peaceful with other dogs

Other Pets: friendly and quite social

Training: intelligent and very trainable

Exercise Needs: very active; daily walk recommended; breed is likely to develop problem behaviors without adequate mental/physical stimulation

Health Conditions: obesity, progressive retinal atrophy, cataracts, hip and elbow dysplasia, anterior cruciate ligament tears, panosteitis, macular corneal dystrophy, myopathy

Lifespan: average 10 to 13 years

2.) Habitat Requirements

Recommended Accessories: dog bed or house with a soft cushion, food/water dishes, toys, collar, leash, harness, grooming supplies

Collar and Harness: sized by weight

Grooming Supplies: narrow-toothed comb, bristle brush, dog nail trimmers

Grooming Frequency: brush 2-3 times a week, especially when molting, bathe only when necessary, or 3-4 times a year in order not to strip the natural oil from their coats, conduct regular examinations of their ears, eyes, teeth and gums, and overall body health

Energy Level: high energy level; lack of exercise can lead to destructive behavior

Exercise Requirements: at least 30 minutes of exercise per day in addition to regular walks

Dog Pillow or Cushion: highly recommended for a large dog since it provides firm support to heavy bones and muscles

Food/Water: stainless steel or ceramic bowls, clean daily

Toys: start with an assortment, see what the dog likes; include some mentally stimulating toys

Exercise Ideas: play games to give your dog extra exercise during the day; swimming, running and fetching are recommended exercises

3.) *Nutritional Needs*

Nutritional Needs: water, protein, carbohydrate, fats, vitamins, minerals

RER: 70 (weight in kg)$^{0.75}$

Calorie Needs: varies by age, weight, and activity level; RER modified with activity level

Amount to Feed (puppy): 4 meals a day, reducing to 3 meals a day after 3 months, and 3 meals after six months, at regular intervals

Amount to Feed (adult): consult recommendations on the package; calculated by weight

Important Ingredients: fresh animal protein (chicken, beef, lamb, turkey, eggs), digestible carbohydrates (rice, oats, barley), animal fats

Important Minerals: calcium, phosphorus, potassium, magnesium, iron, copper and manganese

Important Vitamins: Vitamin A, Vitamin A, Vitamin B-12, Vitamin D, Vitamin C

Look For: AAFCO statement of nutritional adequacy; protein at top of ingredients list; no artificial flavors, dyes, preservatives

4.) Breeding Information

Age of First Heat: around two years old, sometimes earlier

Heat (Estrus) Cycle: 14 to 21 days

Frequency: twice a year, every 6 to 7 months

Greatest Fertility: 11 to 15 days into the cycle

Gestation Period: 59 to 63 days

Pregnancy Detection: possible after 21 days, best to wait 28-30 days before exam

Feeding Pregnant Dogs: maintain normal diet until week 5 or 6 then slightly increase rations by 20 to 50 percent for the last five weeks

Signs of Labor: body temperature drops below normal 100° to 102°F (37.7° to 38.8°C), may be as low as 98°F (36.6°C); dog begins nesting in a dark, quiet place

Contractions: period of 10 minutes in waves of 3 to 5 followed by a period of rest

Whelping: may last for about two to four hours or more, depending on the litter size

Puppies: born with eyes and ears closed; eyes open at 3 weeks, teeth develop at 10 weeks

Litter Size: average 7 to 15 puppies

Size at Birth: about 10 to 16 oz.

Weaning: supplement with controlled portions of moistened puppy food at 3-5 weeks, with water freely available, fully weaned at 5-6 weeks

Socialization: start as early as possible to prevent puppies from being nervous as an adult, preferably before 14-16 weeks of age

Index

D

E

F

R

S

T

U

V

W

Photo Credits

Cover Page Photo By Djmirko via Wikimedia Commons. <https://commons.wikimedia.org/wiki/File:YellowLabradorLooking_new.jpg>

Page 1 Photo By Lefalher via Wikimedia Commons. <https://commons.wikimedia.org/wiki/File:MG_3867_Joucas _20090418.jpg>

Page 7 Photo By Flickr user mrpattersonsir via Wikimedia Commons. <https://commons.wikimedia.org/wiki/File:Black_Labrador_ Retrievers_portrait.jpg>

Page 15 Photo By Pleple2000 via Wikimedia Commons. <https://commons.wikimedia.org/wiki/File:Labrador_czekol adowy757.jpg>

Page 23 Photo by Jared and Corin. <https://www.flickr.com/photos/87434398@N00/113558217> as Uploaded to Wikipedia Commons by Pharaoh Hound. <https://commons.wikimedia.org/wiki/File:Labrador_Retriev er_yellow_puppy.jpg>

Page 31 Photo by J-F Le Falher via Wikimedia Commons. <https://commons.wikimedia.org/wiki/File:021_labrador_ret riever.JPG>

Page 37 Photo by sgilsdorf. <https://www.flickr.com/photos/51913773@N00/780353117>as Uploaded to Wikipedia Commons by Pharaoh Hound. <https://commons.wikimedia.org/wiki/File:Labrador_Retrievers_yellow_and_red.jpg>

Page 43 Photo by Erikeltic via Wikimedia Commons. <https://commons.wikimedia.org/wiki/File:3labradorcols.jpg>

Page 49 Photo by Andrew Skolnick via Wikimedia Commons. <https://commons.wikimedia.org/wiki/File:Wayfield's_Young_Argos,_the_Labrador_Retriever.jpg>

Page 57 Photo by Audrey from USA. <https://www.flickr.com/photos/98799884@N00/458101145/>

Page 65 Photo by IDS photos from Tiverton, IK via Wikimedia Commons. <https://commons.wikimedia.org/wiki/File:Chez_at_Quantock_Show_%282828232459%29.jpg>

Page 69 Photo by Blaine Hansel. <https://www.flickr.com/photos/hansel/9610327/in/set-240322/>

Page 81 Photo by River Retrievers via Wikimedia Commons. <https://commons.wikimedia.org/wiki/File:Silver_Labrador_Puppy.jpg>

References

"An Introduction to Caring for a Labrador Retriever." Mark Jenner. <http://www.labradortraininghq.com/labrador-health-and-care/intro-to-caring-for-a-labrador-retriever/>

"Autosomal Recessive Centronuclear Myopathy in Labrador Retrievers." Animal Health Trust. <http://www.aht.org.uk/cms-display/genetics_myopathy.html>

"Breeding Labrador Retrievers." aquaticcommunity.com. <http://www.aquaticcommunity.com/dog/labrador/breeding.php>

"Breeder's Tools." labradornet.com. <http://labradornet.com/reproduction.html>

"Canine Nutrition Basics." thebark.com. <http://thebark.com/content/canine-nutrition-basics>

"Canine Reproduction." Wikipedia. <https://en.wikipedia.org/wiki/Canine_reproduction>

"Dealing with Cruciate Ligament Injuries in Labrador Retrievers." woodhavenlabs.com <http://www.woodhavenlabs.com/ccl-injuries.html>

"Dental Care For Your Labrador." Pippa.
<http://www.thelabradorsite.com/dental-care-for-your-labrador/>

"Dog licence." Wikipedia.
<https://en.wikipedia.org/wiki/Dog_licence>

"Dog Nutrition Tips." ASPCA. <http://www.aspca.org/pet-care/dog-care/dog-nutrition-tips>

"Feeding a Labrador Puppy - What to Feed and How Much?" Petsworld. <https://www.petsworld.in/blog/feeding-a-labrador-puppy-what-to-feed-and-how-much.html>

"Grooming Your Labrador Retriever." Woodhaven Labradors.
<http://www.woodhavenlabs.com/grooming.html>

"Hereditary Muscle Disease (Non-Inflammatory Myopathy in Labrador Retrievers." PetMd.
<http://www.petmd.com/dog/conditions/musculoskeletal/c_dg_hereditary_noninflammatory_myopathy_in_labrador_retriever>

"Hip Dysplasia in Dogs." MypetMD.
<http://www.petmd.com/dog/conditions/musculoskeletal/c_dg_hip_dysplasia>

"Hip Dysplasia in Dogs: Diagnosis, Treatment, and Prevention." peteducation.com.
<http://www.peteducation.com/article.cfm?c=2+2084&aid=444>

"How Much to Feed a Dog to Meet His Energy Needs."
peteducation.com.
<http://www.peteducation.com/article.cfm?c=2+1659&aid=26
12>

"How to clean dog's ears." Josh Weiss-Roessler.
<https://www.cesarsway.com/dog-care/ear-care/how-to-
clean-dogs-ears>

"Keeping your Labrador Retriever healthy." Julie Perrill.
<http://www.examiner.com/article/keeping-your-labrador-
retriever-healthy>

"Labrador Breed Standard - What Makes a Lab a Lab?"
Labrador Training HQ.
<http://www.labradortraininghq.com/labrador-breed-
information/labrador-breed-
standard/#General_Appearance>

"Labrador Health and Care." Labrador Training HQ.
<http://www.labradortraininghq.com/labrador-health-and-
care/>

"Labrador Health Problems." Pippa.
<http://www.thelabradorsite.com/labrador-health-
problems/>

"Labrador Retriever." dogtime.com.
  <http://dogtime.com/dog-breeds/labrador-retriever>

"Labrador Retriever ." MypetMD.com.
<http://www.petmd.com/dog/breeds/c_dg_labrador_retrie
ver#>

"Labrador Retriever." Sam.
<http://labradorretrieverk10.weebly.com/>

"Labrador Retriever." vetstreet.com.
<http://www.vetstreet.com/dogs/labrador-
retriever#health>

"Labrador Retriever." Wikipedia.
<https://en.wikipedia.org/wiki/Labrador_Retriever>

"Labrador Retriever Health Problems and Raising a
Labrador Retriever Puppy to be Healthy."
yourpurebredpuppy.com.
<http://www.yourpurebredpuppy.com/health/labradorretr
ievers.html>

"Labrador Retriever Patellar Luxation." UFAW.
<http://www.ufaw.org.uk/dogs/labrador-retriever-patellar-
luxation>

"Labrador Retriever Temperament What's Good About 'Em,
What's Bad About 'Em." Michele Welton.
<http://www.yourpurebredpuppy.com/reviews/labradorre
trievers.html>

"Luxating Patella in Labrador Retrievers." Shannon Steffen.
<http://www.8pawsup.com/labrador-retriever-luxating-
patella/>

"Macular Corneal Dystrophy in the Labrador Retriever."
Animal Health Trust. <http://www.aht.org.uk/cms-
display/genetics_macularcornealdystrophy.html>

"People Foods to Avoid Feeding Your Pets." ASPCA.
http://www.aspca.org/pet-care/animal-poison-
control/people-foods-avoid-feeding-your-pets

"Principles of Dog Nutrition." Petmd.com.
<http://www.petmd.com/dog/nutrition/evr_dg_principles_
of_dog_nutrition?page=4>

"Progressive Retinal Atrophy." Eye Care for Animals.
<http://www.eyecareforanimals.com/conditions/progressiv
e-retinal-atrophy/>

"Progressive Retinal Atrophy (PRA) in Dogs." Animal Eye
Care LLC. "
<http://www.eyecareforanimals.com/conditions/progressiv
e-retinal-atrophy/>

"Puppy Proofing Your Home." peteducation.com.
<http://www.peteducation.com/article.cfm?c=2+2106&aid=
3283>

"Reproduction." LabradorNet.
<http://labradornet.com/reproduction.html>

"Retinal Dysplasia in Labradors." justlabradors.com.
<http://www.justlabradors.com/health-and-
nutrition/retinal-dysplasia-labradors>

"Selecting a Puppy." thelabradorclub.com
<http://www.thelabradorclub.com/subpages/show_content
s.php?page=Selecting+A+Puppy>

"Socializing a New Puppy." WebMD.
<http://pets.webmd.com/dogs/guide/socializing-new-
puppy>

"The Cost of Owning a Lab." Labs4rescue.
<http://labs4rescue.com/costs.shtml>

"The Labrador Retriever." Dog Owner's Guide.
<http://www.canismajor.com/dog/labrador.html>

"The Reproductive Cycle in Dogs - a Guide to Dogs in Heat."
<Labrador Retriever Guide. http://www.labrador-retriever-
guide.com/dogsinheat.html>

"The Silver Labrador Retriever Facts and Controversy."
labradortraining.hq.
<http://www.labradortraininghq.com/labrador-breed-
information/silver-labrador-retriever/>

"The Working Labrador Retriever." thelabradorsite.com.
<http://www.thelabradorsite.com/the-working-labrador-
retriever/>

"Weaning Puppies: What do Do." Pets.Webmd.com.
<http://pets.webmd.com/dogs/weaning-puppies-what-do>

"Whelping: New Puppies On the Way!" PetMD. <http://www.petmd.com/dog/puppycenter/health/evr_dg_ whelping_new_puppies_on_the_way?page=2>

Feeding Baby
Cynthia Cherry
978-1941070000

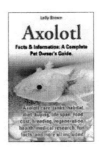

Axolotl
Lolly Brown
978-0989658430

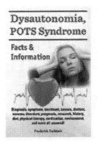

Dysautonomia, POTS
Syndrome
Frederick Earlstein
978-0989658485

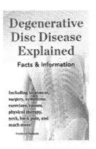

Degenerative Disc
Disease Explained
Frederick Earlstein
978-0989658485

Sinusitis, Hay Fever,
Allergic Rhinitis Explained
Frederick Earlstein
978-1941070024

Wicca
Riley Star
978-1941070130

Zombie Apocalypse
Rex Cutty
978-1941070154

Capybara
Lolly Brown
978-1941070062

Eels As Pets
Lolly Brown
978-1941070167

Scabies and Lice Explained
Frederick Earlstein
978-1941070017

Saltwater Fish As Pets
Lolly Brown
978-0989658461

Torticollis Explained
Frederick Earlstein
978-1941070055

Kennel Cough
Lolly Brown
978-0989658409

Physiotherapist, Physical
Therapist
Christopher Wright
978-0989658492

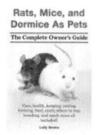

Rats, Mice, and Dormice
As Pets
Lolly Brown
978-1941070079

Wallaby and Wallaroo Care
Lolly Brown
978-1941070031

Bodybuilding Supplements
Explained
Jon Shelton
978-1941070239

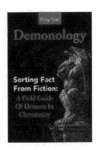

Demonology
Riley Star
978-19401070314

Pigeon Racing
Lolly Brown
978-1941070307

Dwarf Hamster
Lolly Brown
978-1941070390

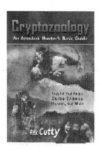

Cryptozoology
Rex Cutty
978-1941070406

Eye Strain
Frederick Earlstein
978-1941070369

Inez The Miniature Elephant
Asher Ray
978-1941070353

Vampire Apocalypse
Rex Cutty
978-1941070321